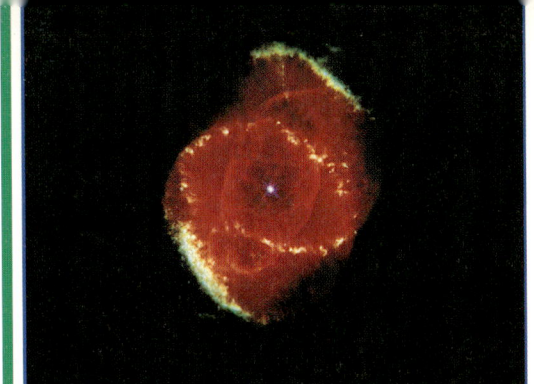

Space Exploration

A Pro/Con Issue

Sarah Flowers

 **Enslow Publishers, Inc.**
40 Industrial Road   PO Box 38
Box 398   Aldershot
Berkeley Heights, NJ 07922   Hants GU12 6BP
USA   UK
http://www.enslow.com

For my mother, who let me be late to school on May 5, 1961, so that I could watch Alan Shepard's flight on TV

Copyright © 2000 by Enslow Publishers, Inc.

All rights reserved.

No part of this book may be reproduced by any means without the written permission of the publisher.

Library of Congress Cataloging-in-Publication Data

Flowers, Sarah, 1952–
Space exploration : a pro/con issue / Sarah Flowers.
     p. cm. — (Hot pro/con issues)
  Includes bibliographical references and index.
  Summary: Examines the debate over whether the United States should continue putting money into its space program.
  ISBN 0-7660-1199-2
    1. Astronautics—United States—Juvenile literature.
2. Outer space—Exploration—United States—Juvenile literature.
3. Astronautics—Economic aspects—Juvenile literature.
4. Technology—Risk assessment—Juvenile literature.
  [1. Astronautics. 2. Outer space—Exploration.] I. Title. II. Series.
TL793.F565   2000
333. 9'4—dc21   98-54613
                                                       CIP
                                                       AC

Printed in the United States of America

10 9 8 7 6 5 4 3 2 1

To Our Readers:
All Internet addresses in this book were active and appropriate when we went to press. Any comments or suggestions can be sent by e-mail to Comments@enslow.com or to the address on the back cover.

Illustration Credits: AP/Wide Word Photos, p. 29; AP/Wide Word Photos and National Aeronautics and Space Administration (NASA), pp. 32, 41; © Corel Corporation, pp. 9, 23, 52; NASA, pp. 1, 4, 16; NASA/JPL, p. 44.

Cover Illustration: NASA

contents

1 Beyond Earth.................. 5

2 The Space Race 14

3 Risks and Costs................ 26

4 Is Space Exploration Worth
Its Risks and Costs? 38

5 The Meaning of
Space Exploration............... 50

Chapter Notes.................. 56

Glossary....................... 61

Further Reading 63

Index 64

Although *Challenger*'s liftoff was successful, it exploded in midair less than two minutes later. All seven people aboard the space shuttle were killed.

Chapter 1

Beyond Earth

On a January day in 1986, schoolchildren all over the United States were allowed to watch television during class. It was a special occasion. New Hampshire teacher Christa McAuliffe was about to become the first ordinary citizen in space. She had been training for months to travel with a crew of six astronauts on board the U.S. space shuttle *Challenger*. She planned to teach a class from space. It was to be broadcast to schools all over the country. But less than two minutes into the flight, *Challenger* exploded in midair, killing all seven on board. It was the most serious failure in the history of United States space travel. It put an end to space shuttle flights for more than two years, until the cause of the explosion could be determined and fixed.[1]

The *Challenger* disaster was certainly not the first disaster in space, nor was it even the first time people died. But it had been a long time since there had been any major problems. Americans had begun to think of the space program as something tame and everyday. The loss of seven people on live television made Americans stop and think. They began to discuss seriously what the future should hold for space exploration.

Why Explore Space?

Why should humans explore space at all? Some people think that we have a natural impulse to explore our world and even beyond. Robert Ballard is the oceanographer who discovered the wreck of the *Titanic* on the ocean floor. He says, "Everyone is an explorer. How could you possibly live your life looking at a door and not go open it?"[2] Space is one of those doors. In 1962, President John F. Kennedy announced his goal to send a man to the Moon and bring him back safely by the end of the decade. In a speech a few weeks later, he answered the question "Why go to the Moon?" He said, "We choose to go to the Moon! We choose to go to the Moon in this decade, and do the other things, not because they are easy, but because they are hard. Because that goal will serve to organize and measure the best of our energies and skills."[3]

Other people have more practical reasons for exploring space. Nations have competed with one another for control of space. In 1958, not long after the Soviet Union sent up its first satellite, U.S. Senate majority leader Lyndon Johnson, who would later become president of the United States, stated, "Control of space means control of the world."[4] During most of the 1960s, much of the country believed it was vitally important for the United States to win the "space race" and get to the Moon before the Soviet Union did. It was a matter of national pride and, to many people, of national safety.

Some people feel that space exploration is

important because it will help us prepare to colonize other worlds. Gregg Maryniak of the Space Studies Institute, a nonprofit organization in Princeton, New Jersey, believes that space colonies are important for Earth's future. According to Maryniak, colonies on the Moon, Mars, or other planets "can supply clean energy necessary for human survival in the twenty-first century. In addition, they can provide new homelands and an expanded ecological niche for our species."[5] Some people fear that if Earth's population continues to grow at current rates, we will need to find other places for people to live—and that means other planets.

Still other people think that the primary purpose of space exploration is to protect Earth's environment. Astronaut Sally Ride says,

> The planet we live on is much more fragile than we thought it was. . . . So it's important to understand the earth's ecosystem on a global scale and how it's changing. The only way we can effectively do that is from space, because that's the only place where we can get a view of the entire planet.[6]

Supporters of this line of thinking believe that the best way to protect Earth's environment is to know as much as possible about it. They believe that space-based observations can help us see what is happening to our planet and what we can do to help it support all of us.

Many people feel that the ultimate goal of space exploration should be to find life on other planets. The Search for Extraterrestrial Intelligence (SETI) is the process by which scientists all over the world are looking for proof of life outside our planet. Astrophysicist Thomas R. McDonough, SETI coordinator for the Planetary Society of Pasadena, California, believes that finding extraterrestrial life is important for humans because it would bring us closer together. He says that we tend to emphasize our national and racial differences. If we learned that there was another civilization somewhere, we could "begin to see ourselves as a single species in which our differences were trivial compared with the differences between us and them."[7] He also believes that if we find another civilization, it may be more advanced than ours. It might be able to offer us solutions to problems such as pollution, overpopulation, and disease.

Other people who believe in space exploration point to the many advances in science that have come directly from the space program. They believe that having a specific goal, such as sending a man to the Moon or a robot to Mars, encourages scientists to do basic research. The research results in developments that have useful applications on Earth. Laser technology, bar code scanners, and new metal alloys are a few of the space-based technologies used every day on Earth.

Fantasy and Reality

Before the twentieth century, the idea of leaving Earth was just a fantasy. By the 1920s, advances in science and technology were bringing the fantasy closer to reality. The first rockets were developed for use as weapons during World War II. In October 1957, the Soviet Union launched the first artificial satellite into orbit around Earth. Less than twelve years later, in July 1969, Americans were walking on the surface of the Moon. In the years since then, space probes have traveled to other planets in our

Beyond Earth

solar system and are on their way beyond. Staffed flights have stayed closer to home, with astronauts learning to live and work in space vehicles that orbit Earth.

The idea of exploring other worlds—the Moon, other planets, other solar systems, other galaxies—is appealing to many people, especially Americans. America was settled by pioneers, many of whom set out on foot across a vast unknown continent. In the same way, modern explorers might cross the unknown territory of space.[8] Popular movies and television shows like *Star Wars* and *Star Trek* give

*S*cientists continue to debate the best way to explore space, while technology allows humans to travel even farther away from Earth.

viewers a picture of what it might be like to meet other civilizations and to travel great distances.

Movies, of course, do not have to deal with some of the realities of space travel. They can create solutions to difficulties that real-life scientists have yet to solve. In the *Star Wars* movies, the character Han Solo puts his spaceship, the *Millennium Falcon*, into "hyperdrive" to travel almost instantly across galaxies. *The Enterprise*, the spaceship from *Star Trek*, goes into "warp speed" to get from one solar system to the next. However, as physics is understood today, powering a spaceship to the speed of light and beyond would require more energy than exists in the universe.[9] Even at the speed of light, it would take more than four years to get to the nearest star and thousands of years to travel to other parts of the

Height of Spacecraft

- ✓ Mercury capsule........................ 10.9 ft (3.3 m)
- ✓ Gemini capsule .... 18.8 ft (5.7 m)
- ✓ Apollo lunar module..................... 23 ft (7 m)
- ✓ Apollo command and service modules...................... 34.5 ft (10.5 m)
- ✓ Soyuz spacecraft .... 23.4 ft (7.1 m)
- ✓ Space Shuttle (length of orbiter)...... 122 ft (37.2 m)

Source: *NASA Space History*, February 24, 1999, <http://spaceflight.nasa.gov/history/index.html> (August 13, 1999).

galaxy. So far, this has limited space exploration to within our own solar system.

Space movies have the right idea, however. We have to look beyond our present ways of doing things. Physicist Robert L. Forward says, "To get to the stars in less than a human lifetime, interstellar vehicles must use some form of 'rocketless rocketry.'"[10] Scientists have looked at several types of spaceship designs that use energy sources available in space, such as solar power. Various designs are technically possible but a long way from reality. They require, as Forward says, "the desire and the commitment to a few decades of difficult and expensive space-engineering work."[11] "Hyperdrive" or "warp speed" would require new discoveries and advances in our understanding of physics.

Movies also do not have to be concerned with how much it costs to explore space. In real life, money for space exploration has come mainly from governments. Most governments are responsible to their people for how they spend money. In the end, it is the people of a country who must decide how the money is spent. If they think it is more important to fund medical research or welfare or the military, then space exploration will get less. People usually like to see some immediate benefit for their money. Space exploration is a long-term prospect. Political leaders are more likely to push for programs that will be completed while they are still in office.

Humans or Robots?

Space exploration has been a combination of staffed and unstaffed—or human and robot—voyages. Sending humans into space is more expensive than sending robots, but it is also more exciting. There are still some things humans can do that robots cannot. But space is naturally dangerous for people. Humans cannot live in space—or on any of the other planets or moons of our solar system—without life-support systems to supply food, water, breathable air, waste disposal, and temperature control. All those things are expensive and take up room. The larger a spacecraft is, the more fuel it requires. According to Alex Roland, a Duke University space historian, the space shuttle "burns nearly two million kilograms [2,200 tons] of expensive fuel just to get into orbit."[12] Smaller spacecraft require smaller rockets and less fuel.

Some people think there is an obvious solution to the problem of bulky and expensive life-support systems. They would not be needed if robotic probes went into space instead of people. Roland points out, "Unlike humans, robots don't have to be fed and they don't get tired." They also do not have lives and families back on Earth, so it does not matter if they never come back.[13]

But robots cannot do everything humans can do. When the *Mars Pathfinder*, a small robot lander, stopped sending signals back from Mars in the fall of 1997, it could not fix itself. Scientists suspect that its battery ran down and disrupted its timing mechanism. A human could have recharged the pack or fixed a minor mechanical problem, but no one was there to do it. In a similar situation, humans on the space shuttle were able to fix a problem that had caused the Hubble Space Telescope to send back blurry pictures. David Brandt of the National Space Society says, "Unlike robots, humans don't have to wait for commands to take action."[14]

Beyond Earth

Exploring New Worlds

Human beings have been exploring for thousands of years. In the past five hundred years, people have visited practically every part of Earth. In the words of astronomer Carl Sagan, "There are now humans on every continent—from pole to pole, from Mount Everest to the Dead Sea—on the ocean bottoms, and in residence 200 miles up in the sky."[15] In the past few decades, we have taken the first steps off our planet and out into the universe beyond. It seems likely that we will continue to explore, because we have dreams and visions of what the future could be like. As Sagan says, "Dreams are maps. . . . It is our responsibility . . . to open up the solar system to those intrepid explorers from planet Earth."[16]

Chapter 2

The Space Race

On October 4, 1957, the Space Age truly began. For the first time, a human-made object left Earth's atmosphere. The Soviet Union launched into orbit a small steel satellite called *Sputnik 1*. The first Sputnik was only 23 inches (58 cm) in diameter and weighed 184 pounds (84 kg).[1] It orbited Earth once every ninety-six minutes, sending back a radio signal so that scientists could track it. The radio signal made a beep-beep noise, and even amateur radio operators could follow *Sputnik's* movement by that signal. A radio announcer in the United States said of the signal, "Until two days ago, that sound has never been heard on this Earth. Suddenly it has become as much a part of twentieth-century life as the whir of your vacuum cleaner."[2]

Another thing that was becoming a part of twentieth-century life was fear. The United States and the Soviet Union (U.S.S.R.) were involved in what was known as a cold war. Neither country trusted the other. Each had a different form of government. Each was convinced that the other wanted to dominate the whole world. The only fighting was with words, not weapons, but people in both countries were suspicious of people in the other. Some Americans were worried that once the Soviets had satellites in space, they could launch a surprise nuclear attack on the United States. Immediately after the *Sputnik* launch, both the U.S. Army and U.S. Air Force began to plan space programs. Within months, however, Congress created a civilian space agency called the National Aeronautics and Space Administration (NASA). Soon, most space activities moved from the military to NASA.

On July 29, 1958, President Eisenhower signed into law the National Aeronautics and Space Act of 1958. The act declared, "It is the policy of the United States that activities in space should be devoted to peaceful purposes for the benefit of all mankind."[3] NASA would plan, direct, and conduct space activities.

Throughout the 1950s and 1960s, the United States and the Soviet Union were involved in what came to be known as the space race. The two countries raced against each other to have firsts—first satellite, first astronaut in space, first space walk, first to land on the Moon. At stake was national pride. Many people saw it as a version of the Cold War: Which would be more successful in space, the Democratic government of the United States or the Communist government of the Soviet Union? Americans saw that the Soviet Union was leading in the race because they had more scientists. John Gunther, a journalist reporting from Russia, noted, "The Soviet child graduating [the equivalent of a U.S. high school], . . . aged about seventeen, has a

Sputnik I, a small steel satellite, was the first human-made object to leave Earth's atmosphere.

better scientific education than most American *college* graduates."⁴ American schools immediately began to improve their science and mathematics programs. Nikita Khrushchev, the leader of the Soviet Union, meanwhile, was determined that "something Soviet would be in orbit every day, to continue to impress the world with the strength of Communism."⁵

Satellites

At first, it seemed as though the Soviet Union would win the race without much competition. A month after *Sputnik 1*, the U.S.S.R. launched a much larger satellite, *Sputnik 2*. It carried the first living creature into space, a dog named Laika. Laika survived the launch and lived for a few days, until her air supply was used up. Her trip showed that it was possible to live through increased gravity during launch and a period of weightlessness while in space.

Meanwhile, the United States attempted to launch a grapefruit-sized satellite on top of a rocket. The first launch was set for December 6, 1957, just a month after *Sputnik 2*. Reporters were invited to the launch, which was intended to show that America was keeping up with the Soviets. Unfortunately, the launch was a total disaster. One eyewitness said that the rocket "hesitated for a moment, quivered again, and in front of our unbelieving, shocked eyes, began to topple. It sank like a great flaming sword down into the blast tube."⁶ It was a serious blow for a country that usually thought of itself as a leader in technology. George R. Reedy, an aide to Senator Lyndon Johnson, said, "The simple fact is that we can no longer consider the Russians to be behind us in technology. It took them four years to catch up to our atomic bomb and nine months to catch up to our hydrogen bomb. Now we are trying to catch up to their satellite."[7]

It was only a few months, however, before the United States had satellites orbiting Earth as well. The first was *Explorer 1*, launched on January 31, 1958. *Explorer 1* was smaller than either of the Sputniks, but it went higher into orbit. It detected a zone of intense radiation that became known as the Van Allen radiation belt. It was the first of many Explorer satellites over the next twenty years. They each contained scientific instruments and sent back huge amounts of information about solar wind, magnetic fields, and ultraviolet radiation. Other satellites followed, and these allowed worldwide television transmissions and other communications, improved weather forecasting, and much more.

Putting Humans in Space

From the beginning of the space race, Soviets and Americans had the goal of putting human beings into space. One of the first official actions of NASA was to approve Project Mercury, the program that would send a man into orbit around Earth. Similarly, the Soviet Union was hard at work on the Vostok program. Both countries planned to start by sending dogs and monkeys into space.

But first they had to find a way to bring a spacecraft safely back to Earth. The early satellites were sent to orbit the planet and were never intended to return. Eventually, they fell back to Earth, burning up as they fell. That was no way to deal with humans. In 1960 the Soviets sent up *Sputnik 5*, which contained two dogs, Belka and

Strelka. The dogs were in a capsule that was of the same design that would later be used to send humans into space. The capsule made eighteen orbits of Earth, then returned safely, with Belka and Strelka alive and well.[8] Other capsules burned up on reentry with their canine passengers. By March 1961, however, the Soviets had made several successful rescues. It was clear that the Soviet

Program	Number of Flights	Number of Crew Members	Days in Space
U.S. Mercury	6	6	2
U.S. Gemini	10	20	38
U.S. Apollo	11	33	104
U.S. Skylab	3	9	172
U.S. Apollo-Soyuz Test	1	3	9
U.S. Space Shuttle	95	573	811
U.S.S.R. Vostok	6	6	13
U.S.S.R. Voskhod	2	5	2
U.S.S.R. Soyuz	36	73	825
U.S.S.R. Soyuz-T	13	34	903

Sources: "Nasa Space Shuttle," *Nasa Human Spaceflight*, July 29, 1999 <http://spaceflight.nasa.gov/shuttle/archives> (August 31, 1999); Philip Clark, *The Soviet Manned Space Program* (New York: Orion Books, 1988); "U.S. Human Space Flight Log" *Nasa Human Spaceflight: Astronaut Fact Book*, n.d., <http://www.shuttle.nasa.gov/spacenews/factsheets/pdfs/np199807008jsc.pdf> (August 31, 1999); Valerie Neal et al., *Spaceflight: A Smithsonian Guide* (New York: Macmillan, 1995).

Union was getting close to being able to send a human into space.

The United States, meanwhile, was doing similar experiments with animals, including mice and monkeys. In January 1961, a Mercury capsule was launched carrying a chimpanzee named Ham. The capsule did not go into orbit, but it did leave the atmosphere and return safely.

The Soviet Union won this part of the space race. On April 12, 1961, Yuri Gagarin of the Soviet Union became the first man in space. Both the Soviets and the Americans had been training pilots to fly spacecraft. The early flights involved very little human piloting, but both countries decided that the best-qualified people would be military test pilots. These pilots had experience flying at high speeds and high altitudes. They were trained to evaluate risks and to think quickly in stressful situations. Gagarin was a Soviet Air Force pilot.

Before he climbed into the rocket that would lift him into space and into history, Gagarin expressed a view that could be understood by explorers of all times and places. He said, "To be the first to enter the cosmos, to engage, single-handed, in an unprecedented duel with nature—could one dream of anything more?"[9] Gagarin's Vostok spacecraft made one orbit of Earth and spent just under two hours in space.

Less than a month later, on May 5, 1961, Alan Shepard became the first American in space. His flight, part of Project Mercury, did not orbit Earth. It went up to a distance of 116.5 miles. Then the capsule automatically repositioned itself with its heat shield down and reentered the atmosphere. Television and radio stations provided live coverage of the event. The whole trip lasted about fifteen minutes.

Humans to the Moon

Three weeks after Alan Shepard's flight, President John F. Kennedy called on Congress to take a "leading role in space achievement." He said, "I believe that this nation should commit itself to achieving the goal, before this decade is out, of landing a man on the moon and returning him safely to earth."[10] During the next eight years, the United States government concentrated on accomplishing that goal. NASA's portion of the federal budget climbed from one percent in 1959 to 4 percent in 1965. NASA hired the best scientists and engineers to develop and build its space program.

Project Mercury was followed by Project Gemini, in which two men at a time went into space. The Gemini program achieved the first successful docking of two space vehicles. In docking, two separate spacecraft had to be maneuvered together and attached. The ability to dock two craft in space would be crucial to a moon landing.

Meanwhile, the Soviets sent the first woman, Valentina Tereshkova, into space on June 16, 1963. In 1964, they started sending two or three cosmonauts at a time into space. In 1965, Alexei Leonov became the first human to "walk" in space, venturing outside his spacecraft. It was an exciting and bold event. Space walks, or extravehicular activity (EVA), would be essential to the space program. It would be necessary to leave a spacecraft to walk on the Moon. EVA would also allow astronauts to mend a damaged spacecraft, to rescue a stranded astronaut, or to build a space station. Leonov's space walk proved that a space suit was enough protection and life support for a human in space.[11]

The Gemini program in the United States was immediately followed by the Apollo program, in which three-man crews prepared to go to the Moon. In December of 1968, James Lovell, Frank Borman, and William Anders became the first humans to orbit the Moon. Seven months later, on July 20, 1969, Neil Armstrong and Buzz Aldrin became the first to walk on the surface of the Moon.

The Apollo program continued for a few more years. Apollo crews brought back samples of moon rocks and experimented with a lunar rover vehicle. After the Moon landing, though, both public interest and government support declined. NASA's budget share shrank, and proposed flights were canceled.

Meanwhile, the Soviet Union had begun to look at long-term missions in space. In 1971 they launched their *Salyut 1*, a space station. All through the 1970s and 1980s, they sent cosmonauts to spend longer periods of time on the space station. In 1986 they launched the *Mir* space station and occupied it continuously until 1999. The United States had a space station called *Skylab*, but its orbit decayed and it fell to Earth in 1979. The United States turned to the space shuttle program. The shuttle was intended to be an easily reusable spacecraft. Astronauts used the shuttle to perform experiments in space.

Unstaffed Programs

The United States and Soviet Union also sent unstaffed space probes to explore the other planets in the solar system. The Soviets sent a series of

*O*n July 20, 1969, Neil Armstrong and Buzz Aldrin became the first humans to walk on the Moon. Here, Aldrin descends from the lunar module on a ladder.

Venera probes to explore Venus during the 1960s, 1970s, and early 1980s. The probes sent back detailed information about the planet's surface and atmosphere. The Soviets also had a series of Mars probes, only one of which successfully returned data from the planet.

The United States eventually sent probes to all the planets in the solar system except Pluto. Pluto's distance, position, and orbit made a probe impractical. The Mariner probes explored Venus, Mercury, and Mars. The Pioneer Venus and Magellan probes mapped the surface of Venus. In the 1970s, two Viking probes landed on Mars and sent back pictures that confirmed the reddish color of that planet's surface. In 1972, *Pioneer 10* went to Jupiter, where it sent back the first close-up photographs of the giant planet. Then it used Jupiter's gravity to fling itself out of Jupiter's orbit and head for the far reaches of the solar system. In March 1997, NASA formally ended the mission, but scientists have hopes that the probe will continue out of the solar system on its way to Aldebaran, a star that is sixty-eight light-years away.[12] Meanwhile, two Voyager probes made a "grand tour" of the outer planets. They sent back detailed information about the asteroid belt, Jupiter, Saturn, and Uranus. Then they passed Pluto on their way out of the solar system. The Pioneer and Voyager probes carry information about Earth in case they are ever intercepted by another intelligent species.

In recent years, the United States has returned to planetary exploration. *Galileo* went to Jupiter in the early 1990s. This probe witnessed the impact of the Shoemaker-Levy comet into Jupiter's surface. The Mars *Observer* left for Mars in 1992, but unfortunately it stopped sending data when it entered the atmosphere of Mars in 1993. More successfully, the *Mars Pathfinder* and its lander, *Sojourner*, sent back detailed pictures of Mars in 1997. In late 1997, the *Cassini* probe was launched, due to arrive at Saturn in 2004. Also launched in late 1997, the *Mars Global Surveyor* began sending back detailed pictures of the surface of that planet in 1998. In January 1999, another Mars probe, the *Polar Lander*, left Earth.

Chapter 3

Risks and Costs

The 1986 *Challenger* explosion was tragic, but it was not the first space disaster. The early days of the space program saw a number of failures and some loss of life. Many of the early unstaffed rocket launches were failures, and millions of dollars of equipment went up in smoke. In October 1960, more than a hundred Soviet rocket scientists and engineers died while watching an experimental rocket launch. They were testing a new kind of propellant, which included nitric acid. A bad connection in the wiring caused a spark that ignited the engine. The explosion killed many of the observers. Then the nitric acid created a toxic cloud that killed even more.[1] It was a tremendous blow to the Soviet rocket program.

In June 1971 a Soviet Soyuz spacecraft prepared to reenter Earth's atmosphere. A valve opened, releasing the air from the cabin into space. The crew members were not wearing pressure suits, and they died in the vacuum of space. Their bodies were recovered when the spacecraft landed. After that, all cosmonauts wore space suits for takeoff and

Risks and Costs

reentry. To make room for the extra supplies, the Soyuz became a two-person instead of a three-person craft.[2]

Americans had disasters and near disasters as well. In January 1967, the first three-man Apollo crew was training in their spacecraft when they smelled something burning. Faulty wiring had set off a spark that ignited in the oxygen-rich atmosphere of the capsule. A fire erupted in the capsule within seconds, and the astronauts could not get the hatch open quickly enough to escape. Virgil "Gus" Grissom, Edward White, and Roger Chafee died of asphyxiation, becoming the first United States space program fatalities.[3] The astronauts had known that their job was hazardous, but until then things had gone well, and everyone was shocked. NASA administrator James Webb said, "We've always known that something like this was going to happen sooner or later. . . . Who would have thought that the first tragedy would be on the ground?"[4] NASA engineers changed the capsule to make it safer, more fireproof, and easier to escape.

Other incidents revealed safety problems but were resolved without any deaths. The *Apollo 13* mission in April 1970 was halfway to the Moon when an explosion ruptured an oxygen tank. The command module had no power, water, or oxygen. It could have been a disaster, but the astronauts were able to use the lunar module as a sort of lifeboat and get back to Earth alive. NASA issued the following statement about the mission:

> *Apollo 13* must officially be classed as a failure. . . . But in another sense, as a brilliant demonstration of the human capability under almost unbearable

stress, it has to be the most successful failure in the annals of space flight.[5]

The 1986 *Challenger* disaster halted United States space shuttle flights for several years. In the 1990s, the Russian space station *Mir* had a series of problems, including a fire, a cooling system leak, power failures, and a collision with a cargo ship.[6]

Both the American and the Soviet space programs have so far survived disasters and mishaps. Both continue to have successful missions. But some people question whether space exploration is worth the cost of even one life. Marcia Smith, a space specialist with the Congressional Research Service, says, "The country really needs to decide if we're willing to take these risks or not."[7] Daniel Goldin, NASA administrator, says, "We're not going to do things that will be unsafe. But life is tough, and if you don't take risks, you don't learn."[8]

What Else Can Go Wrong?

In October 1997 NASA launched the *Cassini* probe, designed to reach Saturn in 2004 and spend four years exploring the planet, its rings, and most of its eighteen or more moons. The launch went smoothly and sent *Cassini* on its way without a hitch. But before the launch, many people were concerned. If something went wrong and the craft exploded on launch, it could have polluted Earth with radioactive plutonium. *Cassini* carries seventy-two pounds of plutonium-238, which is being used to power the craft's batteries during its long journey to Saturn. Plutonium-238 is a radioactive material that is highly poisonous to humans.

In August 1999, *Cassini* swung back by Earth. It used Earth's gravity to give it a boost toward Saturn.

Cassini's fifteen-year mission includes a study of Saturn. Here, engineers and technicians lower the 3,420-pound spacecraft into a launch-vehicle adapter.

Some people were still worried that even the smallest of problems could cause the probe to break apart and release toxic plutonium all over the Earth. Dr. Helen Caldicott, founder of Physicians for Social Responsibility, was one of the people opposed to *Cassini*'s plutonium load. She said, "One pound [of plutonium-238], if uniformly distributed, could hypothetically induce lung cancer in every person on Earth."[9] NASA scientists dispute these figures.

NASA engineers felt confident that the risk was tiny, and they were pleased that there were no problems with the fly-by. They say that even if the craft had re-entered Earth's atmosphere, the plutonium would have been unlikely to contaminate the atmosphere. The plutonium is contained inside small ceramic pellets and cannot be inhaled. Each pellet is wrapped in a very hard metal called iridium. Iridium does not break apart easily, and it melts at only very high temperatures. They feel that the risks involved are far outweighed by the benefits of the information that *Cassini* will send back about Saturn and its moons. They hope the information will help them understand how the planets were formed. They also believe that conditions on Saturn's moon Titan are similar to those that were on Earth millions of years ago. Thus, scientists hope to learn not only about Titan but also about the history of our own planet.[10]

Health

When sixteenth-century European explorers arrived in the Americas, they brought with them germs that caused devastating diseases among the native populations. Over many years, Europeans and

Risks and Costs

Asians had developed immunities to diseases such as smallpox, measles, and typhus. Even if they got the diseases, they did not usually die from them. The American Indians had no such immunities. Smallpox and measles killed millions of them in the first century after contact with European and Asian cultures. Similarly, Europeans brought back syphilis from the Americas, and it infected millions in Europe and Asia. Some people are concerned that by traveling to other planets, even to those within our solar system, we may bring back microbes that will cause new diseases. So far this has not happened, since humans have not traveled any farther than the Moon. Still, it must be part of any discussion about travel to other planets.

The health problems that exist right now have to do with long-term stays in space. The human body loses muscle mass and bone calcium during long periods in zero gravity. With astronauts spending six months and more at a time on space stations, this becomes a significant issue. On September 26, 1996, astronaut Shannon Lucid landed after spending 188 days on *Mir*. She was so weak that she needed help walking to a waiting stretcher.[11] Muscle mass is easy to rebuild, but research has shown that "at least some bone loss from weightlessness is irreversible."[12]

Other issues pose even greater problems. One is solar radiation. At orbiting distance from Earth, the atmosphere is still thick enough to provide some protection. But a trip to Mars, for example, would take people beyond that protective atmosphere. One Canadian scientist projects that "the cumulative radiation would reach critical levels for humans just two to three months after leaving Earth."[13]

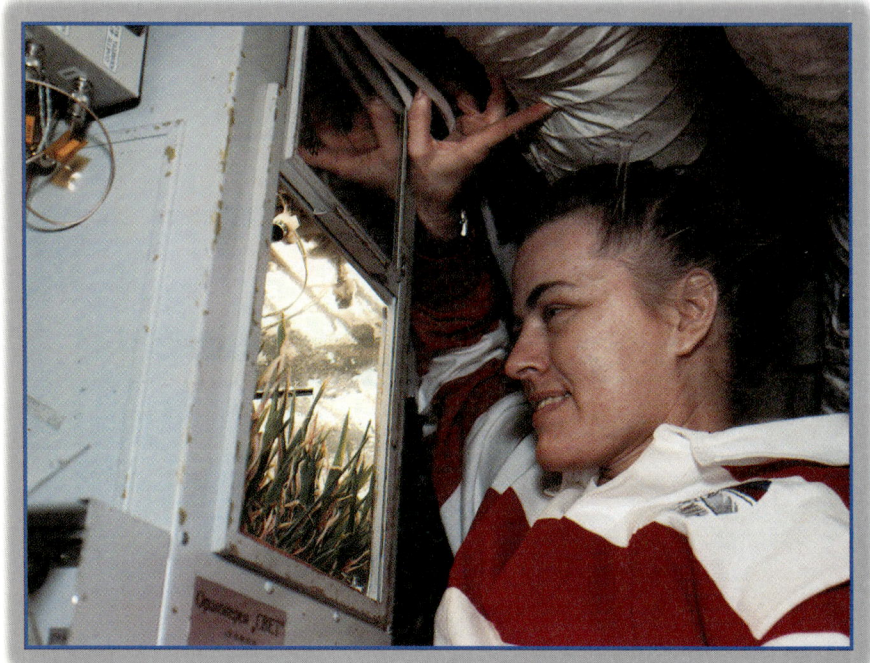

*A*stronaut Shannon Lucid's 188-day stay in space was the longest in history. Here, Lucid inspects an experiment on wheat plants being conducted aboard *Mir*.

Another problem is sleep disruption. There appears to be a link between sleep and the human immune system, but no one is quite sure what the relationship is. Dr. Robert Stickgold of Harvard Medical School notes, "Humans, including their programmed sleep patterns, have evolved according to conditions on Earth," but space is very different.[14] Night and day occur every ninety minutes for someone orbiting Earth in a space station. That, along with boredom, isolation, and stress, affects sleep patterns. Also, dreams are affected by zero gravity, and dreaming is an important part of sleep.

The human immune system can be affected by many factors, including stress and lack of sleep. Space travel currently involves both. Canadian

Risks and Costs

scientist Dr. Harvey Moldofsky believes we need more study on how space travel might affect the immune system. He notes that space travelers bring along with them things from Earth: "bugs, all kinds of bacteria. And so what's happening to these microbes? What's happening with them being bombarded by radiation? And what's the risk of disease and infection?"[15] All of these issues need to be explored in depth before people plan missions that would involve spending years at a time in space.

Life Support

The most obvious physical danger of space is its lack of basic human life support. Space does not contain air or any other natural resource people need to survive. No known planet besides Earth contains those things, either. If people want to travel long distances in space or live on other planets, they will have to find ways to bring or make life-support systems. People need food and water. They also need an atmosphere that is not too hot or too cold. They need air that is not poisonous to them and that is not so heavy it crushes them. When the sixteenth-century explorers traveled across the oceans to new lands, they could stop and find water and food. If necessary, they could even build new ships to take them farther. Because it is not practical to carry enough life-support equipment for a journey of months or years, people must find ways to make what they need as they go along.

Space Junk

Space holds another great danger, and people created this one. Ever since the 1957 launch of

Sputnik 1, we have been hurling satellites and other craft into orbit around Earth. Over the years, some of those items have fallen back to Earth. Most burn up in the atmosphere or fall harmlessly into the oceans. But there is still a lot of junk floating around in space. There are large objects like satellites and rocket boosters. There are also leftovers from flights, including lens caps, bolts, and paint chips.[16] The U.S. Space Command, an office of the U.S. Air Force, tracks all items that are softball-sized or larger. They try to predict when an object might reenter Earth's atmosphere. They inform NASA when objects may interfere with a space shuttle's orbit.

Even very small objects could harm astronauts working outside their spaceships. "A paint chip one millimeter in diameter traveling at 10 kilometers per second could easily tear a hole in a space suit. If the astronaut survives the impact, the resulting pressure loss is still very dangerous."[17] There is a lot of room in space, and the chances so far are minimal of being struck by a piece of space junk. However, increased space activity will only create more junk. One solution would be to shift the debris from current orbits into disposal orbits. These orbits would be at different levels from the orbits of functioning spacecraft. Another idea is to create a space garbage truck to collect some of the debris. So far, those ideas have proven to be too expensive to try.[18]

Is Money Better Spent on Earth?

The expense of space exploration has always seemed to some people like wasted money. They believe the money could be better spent right here on Earth. In a 1998 Gallup poll, 36 percent of those

What Is in Space?

Country	Satellites	Space Probes	Pieces of Debris	Total
USA	718	45	3,129	3,892
USSR/Russia	1,337	35	2,596	3,968
European Space Agency	24	2	228	254
People's Republic of China	26	0	103	129
Japan	65	4	52	121
All Others	439	3	35	477
Total	2,609	89	6,143	8,841

Source: "Satellite Boxscore," *United States Space Command*, July 7, 1999, <http://www.spacecom.af.mil/usspace/boxscore.htm> (August 13, 1999).

surveyed said that they do not believe the space program has brought enough benefits to justify its costs. Space exploration has typically received a small portion (about 1 percent) of the United States budget. For some people, even that is too much. It is money that could be spent improving health care or education or on feeding the hungry, they say.

From the earliest days of the United States space program, some people have been against having the government spend money on space science. In the 1960s, J. William Fulbright, Democratic representative from Arkansas, said that the real question was one of priorities. He believed we were spending too much on weapons and space and too little on education and jobs. At the same time, Joseph Clark,

Space Exploration

Democratic senator from Pennsylvania, said that it was more important for the country to deal with social programs than to go to space.[19]

James Lovell, a former astronaut, disagrees. He says that critics mean well, but they "are wrong when they say we should eliminate space programs to focus on the problems here on Earth. I say space helps us solve those problems."[20] Lovell and others believe that we must look to the future for solutions to Earth's problems. That future must include space.

Most people would agree that human spaceflight is risky. Even robot craft can have problems and

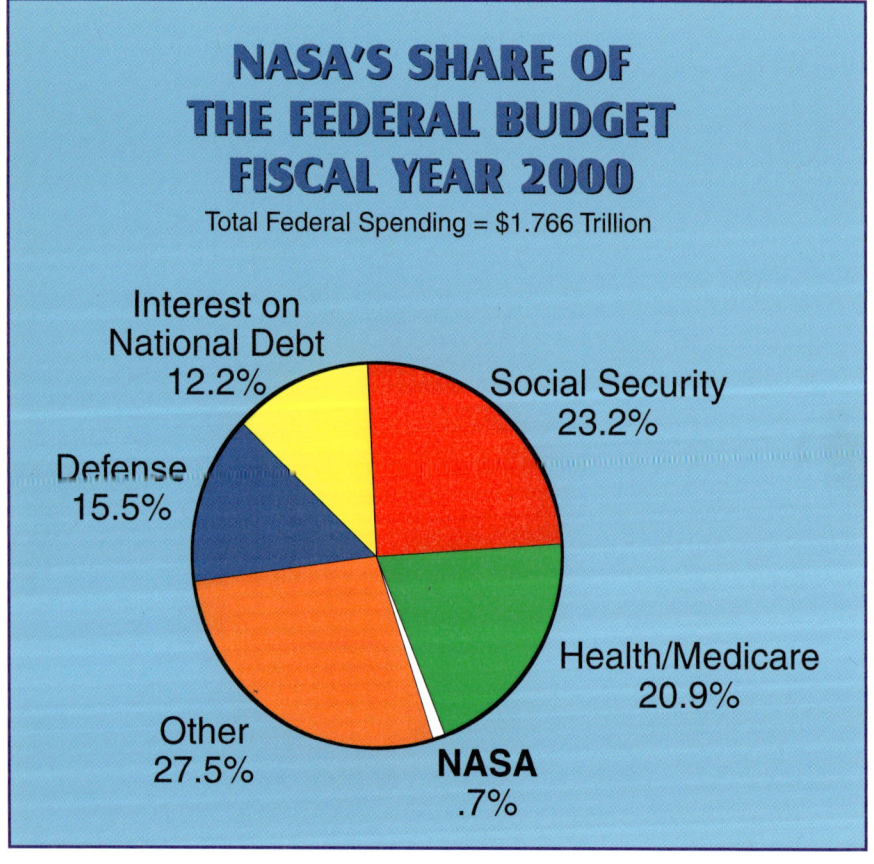

Source: "A Citizen's Guide to the Federal Budget, Fiscal Year 2000," Chart 2-3, n.d., <http://www.access.gpo.gov/usbudget/fy2000/guidetoc.html> (August 31, 1999).

seem like a waste of money. But Eric Chaisson, a scientist who worked on the Hubble Space Telescope, says that all such projects are very complex, and "with complexity comes risk." He says we have to decide how much risk is acceptable. If we want absolutely no element of risk, testing and preparing becomes "impossibly expensive." If we take too many risks, we waste money and lives. Chaisson says we need to find a middle ground, because "risk-taking is a hallmark of all civilizations that become great—they become great partly because they occupy new ground, achieve victory, and accomplish notably new things."

Chapter 4

Is Space Exploration Worth Its Risks and Costs?

The space race of the 1960s had a number of benefits for the United States, the U.S.S.R., and the world. For the United States and the U.S.S.R., the successes and advances were matters of national pride. Spaceflights were shown on television and discussed in newspapers and magazines. Americans generally regarded NASA and the space program as proof that government could work well.

On a more practical level, space technology has had many useful applications on Earth. The aluminum-coated fabric created for space suits led to Earth-bound uses such as survival blankets and wraps for water heaters. Materials designed to be strong but light are used in common items such as bicycle helmets and tennis rackets. Quartz timing crystals, which are used today in wristwatches and small clocks, were first designed for NASA. The bar codes now used everywhere from supermarkets to libraries were first developed so that NASA could keep an accurate inventory of spacecraft parts.

Sophisticated medical imaging technologies such as CAT scans and MRIs are spinoffs from space program technology.[1]

A New Vision

The *Apollo 17* astronauts in 1972 took a famous photograph of Earth as seen from the Moon. That photograph shows the planet with blue seas, white clouds, and brown continental masses. Writer Norman Cousins said in 1976 that the greatest achievement of the Apollo program was "not that man set foot on the Moon, but that he set eye on the Earth." For the first time, people were able to see Earth "small and whole," not "divided by artificial boundaries."[2] President Jimmy Carter expressed the feelings of many when he said,

> From the perspective of space our planet has no national boundaries. It is very beautiful, but it is also very fragile. And it is the special responsibility of the human race to preserve it.[3]

The space program gave the people of Earth a new vision of the planet. For anyone born since 1968, photographs of Earth from space have always been a part of life. But seeing actual photographs of the whole Earth for the first time was a startling and moving experience for those old enough to remember it. The astronauts were only the first of many humans to express their surprise that from space, Earth looked "just like the maps." Before the space program, we "could draw the Earth's surface at any scale or detail, but no one had ever seen the entire planet for the simplest of . . . reasons: we could not get far enough away."[4] The space race may have started as a Cold War battle, but its true success was in making the world a smaller place for all its residents.

International Cooperation

At the beginning of the twenty-first century, space exploration is no longer a race. Many people see it as a chance for different countries to work together. Each can provide one piece of the total effort. The first major cooperative space effort is the International Space Station (ISS). When it is completed, it will orbit Earth 220 miles up. It will be 290 feet (79.9 meters) long, with a wingspan of 356 feet (109 meters) and a weight of nearly a million pounds. In 1998, astronauts from the United States, Russia, and other countries began to carry pieces of the ISS into space on the space shuttle and Soyuz craft and assemble them there.

Many people see the ISS as the wave of the future. With the fall of communism in 1989 and the breakup of the U.S.S.R. in 1991, the Russian Republic took over the Soviet space program. The Cold War is over, and the Russians have been agreeable to working with the United States and other countries to advance space exploration. Because of their *Sulyut* and *Mir* space stations, the Russians have a lot of practice living and working in space.

Why a Space Station?

The United States has joined in the International Space Station project for several reasons, which range from the political to the practical to the inspirational. NASA intends to use the ISS to conduct various kinds of experiments in space. Researchers hope to make advances in life sciences, medical research, and industrial materials. They believe that

This artistic conception of the proposed International Space Station shows a base system and special manipulator arm.

the gravity-free environment of space will help them to develop these new materials and methods.

The United States also sees the ISS as a way to create new partnerships with other nations. NASA believes that breakthroughs and technologies developed in space will have immediate, practical applications on Earth and will create jobs. Additionally, backers of the ISS hope that it will "inspire our children, foster the next generation of scientists, engineers, and entrepreneurs, and satisfy humanity's ancient need to explore and achieve."[5]

The ISS may be an example of the way in which the world has become a "global village" in the years since humans first left the planet in 1961. NASA administrator Daniel Goldin believes that the space station gives us a special opportunity. He says, "The ISS will be a world community living and working together in space, improving life on Earth and expanding humanity's horizons for the twenty-first century."[6]

Learning More About the Solar System

Some people think that the Moon is a natural starting place for further exploration of space. In 1998, a robot spaceship called *Lunar Prospector* detected large amounts of frozen water in the soil of the north and south poles of the Moon. Dr. Alan Binder, a NASA scientist, said, "It means human life can expand to the Moon!" If the ice can be removed from the soil, it could provide water to support human life on the Moon. It could also be broken down into hydrogen and oxygen, which can be used for rocket fuel. Water and fuel supplies would not have to be carried from Earth.

Less than a year earlier, another robot spaceship created excitement when it sent back pictures of the dusty red landscape of Mars. From July of 1997 until September, when it stopped sending images, the *Mars Pathfinder* lander and its *Sojourner* robot rover became as familiar to many Americans as their favorite television characters. Scientists talked about the rocks on Mars nicknamed "Yogi Bear," "Barnacle Bill," and "Casper." Millions of people the world over watched the images of Mars on television or on the Internet and wondered if it would ever be possible for humans to travel to our neighboring planet. The successes of *Lunar Prospector* and *Mars Pathfinder* have renewed interest in exploring beyond Earth.

Better, Faster, Cheaper—and Smaller

On December 4, 1992, astronomer Carl Sagan and NASA administrator Daniel Goldin presented a forum at the California Institute of Technology on the future of America's space program. As they discussed the expense of space exploration, Goldin offered what he called "an extreme position" and suggested that future spaceships should be limited to a weight of 500 pounds and that the time to design and build them should not exceed five years.[7] At that time, neither the *Mars Pathfinder* nor the *Lunar Prospector* was even on the drawing board yet. Five years later, both performed their missions of exploration, fulfilling a new NASA mission to build spacecraft "better, faster, cheaper."

The *Lunar Prospector*, for example, cost about $63 million for the entire mission. The spacecraft itself is about four feet high and weighs about 650

*T*he *Mars Pathfinder* sent many images of the dusty red landscape of Mars back to Earth.

Is Space Exploration Worth Its Risks and Costs?

pounds and was built from existing hardware. The mission manager, Scott Hubbard, said, "We wanted to show that for the cost of a typical Hollywood movie, you can explore interplanetary space."[8] (For comparison, it cost over $200 million to make the 1997 hit movie *Titanic* and $90 million to make *Men in Black*.)

NASA began its New Millennium Program in 1994 to create what they refer to as microcraft. These tiny space probes would be affordable and plentiful. NASA envisions launching ten to fifteen microcraft each year to explore "Earth, the solar system and astrophysical events in and far beyond the Milky Way galaxy."[9] Key to this mission is the development of tiny sensors and other instruments, including a wireless digital camera the size of two sugar cubes.

Imagine a spacecraft the size of a toaster oven and weighing only about twelve pounds (5.5 kilograms). It would use only five watts of power and travel a billion miles away but still be able to send data back to Earth. It would be able to figure out its location and navigate itself, just as the explorers of the sixteenth century did—by looking at the position of the stars. Of course, a spacecraft that small could not carry a human, but many people believe it will be the spacecraft of the future for exploration in and beyond the solar system.

First, though, we need new ways to make parts smaller. We also need new inventions in electronics. And there is still the question of how we can move objects rapidly through space. All these goals require a commitment to do the basic research and to spend the money necessary.

Space Exploration

Commercial Uses of Space

The first sponsors of space exploration, like the first sponsors of ocean exploration, were nations. But it did not take long for private companies to start sending out their own ships, like the Dutch East India Company in the seventeenth century, to take advantage of the trade in spices and tea. Today, private companies are beginning to consider how they can make money in space. Some are looking toward a future in which ordinary citizens can vacation in space. Still others imagine a colony on the Moon or on Mars. Everyone seems to agree that the possibilities are numerous.

At least one company plans to make money by taking tourists into space. According to a 1997 national survey, 42 percent of Americans would consider taking a space cruise and would be willing to spend $10,000 or more for the privilege.[10] Two adventure companies are already taking orders for tickets for suborbital flights. Passengers would go to a height of about sixty-two miles and be weightless for about two and a half minutes before returning to Earth. The ticket price: $98,000. But a former NASA official says that before anyone can seriously consider a space vacation, "space travel must be made a hundred times cheaper, a hundred times more reliable, and a hundred times more regular."[11]

Still, many scientists and businesspeople believe that space tourism is a strong possibility for the future. A NASA spokesperson predicted in 1997 that this sort of space travel "is about ten or fifteen years away if NASA and the private sector develop the research and technology necessary for space tourism."[12] Former astronaut Buzz Aldrin, the

How Americans Rate the Space Program

How would you rate the job being done by NASA?

- ✓ Excellent 26%
- ✓ Good 50%
- ✓ Only fair 17%
- ✓ Poor 4%
- ✓ No opinion 3%

Should the United States space program concentrate on unmanned missions like *Voyager 2*, or should we concentrate on maintaining a manned space program like the space shuttle and space station?

- ✓ Manned missions 52%
- ✓ Unmanned missions 32%
- ✓ Neither/Both 10%
- ✓ No opinion 6%

It is now almost thirty years since the United States first landed men on the moon. Do you think the space program has brought enough benefits to this country to justify its costs?

- ✓ Yes, brought enough benefits 58%
- ✓ No, does not justify its costs 36%
- ✓ No opinion 6%

Source: Frank Newport, "Space Program Gets Positive Reviews From Public," *The Gallup Organization*, December 5, 1998, <http://www.gallup.com/poll/releases/pr981205.asp> (August 13, 1999).

second man to walk on the Moon, agrees. He thinks scientists need to come up with ways to make spaceflight easier on the body. But, he says, "We have amusement rides now that are much more stressful than spaceflight will be."[13]

Other businesspeople are thinking of ways to make money from space. A Colorado man named James Benson has created a company called SpaceDev. He has plans to build a spacecraft and send it to a not-too-distant asteroid. He would make money by selling cargo space to scientists who want to fly experiments to the asteroid. He also has plans to mine the asteroid for minerals like gold and platinum. Benson hopes to make money selling the minerals on Earth. He also looks to the lessons of the nineteenth-century gold rushes: "While the prospectors failed to get rich, the barons who owned the trains and coaches that took them out West made a bundle."[14]

Meanwhile, other entrepreneurs have come up with more ideas for making money in space. Package-delivery companies are investigating the possibilities of shortening delivery times by using space. Other companies are looking at ways to build reusable rockets and selling space on them to firms who want to send up communications satellites. Yet another company, LunaCorp, wants to send a robot rover to the Moon and sell people the opportunity to operate it by remote control.[15]

NASA is not at all opposed to these private schemes to use space. In fact, NASA administrator Daniel Goldin wants to cut NASA spending by getting it out of the business of building huge rockets and spacecraft. He says he wants to "convince private industry that space can be very profitable."[16] Private

Is Space Exploration Worth Its Risks and Costs?

companies would be willing to invest in space technology if they could be convinced that it will have practical and moneymaking uses for them on Earth. For many of these companies, the profit they make is the only thing space exploration means to them. For other people, however, space exploration means different things.

Chapter 5

The Meaning of Space Exploration

In the forty years since humans began to explore space, people have gone to the Moon and spent thousands of hours orbiting Earth, learning to live and work in space. Robot ships have explored the Sun and most of the planets in the solar system. What will be the next space accomplishments? It depends upon the people of the world and how they want to invest their time and money.

Some people believe that we have not yet done any serious space exploration. Neil de Grasse Tyson, director of New York City's Hayden Planetarium, points out that nine times between 1968 and 1972, astronauts visited the Moon. "Otherwise," he says, "when NASA sends astronauts into 'space,' a crew is launched into Earth orbit a few hundred miles above our 8,000-mile-diameter planet. Space travel, this isn't."[1] Tyson says that people will never be willing to spend large amounts of money for exploration for its own sake.

Other people believe that we must explore

The Meaning of Space Exploration

space and look for other planets. Walter Kistler, president of Foundation for the Future, says, "Exploring space and colonizing other planets is not an option. It is a necessity if humanity is to evolve and not become a stagnant species."[2] Tyson, on the other hand, says that even if we have all the money we need and all the desire in the world, it may not be enough. "What we need, but may never have," he says, "is a breakthrough in our scientific understanding of the structure of the universe."[3] He believes that we must find some kind of "shortcut" through space. Otherwise, it will take us too long to get anywhere.

Other Planets

For years people have wondered whether planets exist outside our solar system. Science-fiction books and movies have imagined what it might be like to meet people from another planet. It is impossible to know what creatures from another planet would look like or how they would act. It is almost as hard to imagine that Earth holds the only life anywhere among the billions of stars in the universe. Until the past few years, however, there was not even any proof that there were planets outside our solar system.

Between 1995 and 1998, astronomers found seventeen planets in other solar systems. Better telescopes, including the Hubble Space Telescope, have helped scientists find these planets. So far, the planets that have been found are not anything like Earth. In fact, astronomers still do not agree that any other Earth-like planets exist anywhere. Some believe that there is nothing like our solar system anywhere in the universe. Others, according to

When a malfunction caused the Hubble Space Telescope to transmit blurry pictures, astronauts on the space shuttle were able to fix the problem.

The Meaning of Space Exploration

University of Hawaii astronomer Bradford Smith, "believe that when you form stars you form planets at the same time."[4] They think there might be many Earth-like planets in our galaxy and beyond. "The problem," says Smith, "is [that] Earth-like planets are small and . . . much more difficult to detect."[5]

Getting to any of those other planets, though, is an even harder task. Gerard O'Neill, a physics professor at Princeton University, says that the only way to do it will be to have large colonies of people traveling in huge "space islands." Because the journey would take years, the colonists would have to be put into a state of suspended animation.[6] Before that can happen, scientists will have to find ways to keep people alive in that state for long periods of time, then revive them when they approached a livable planet.

Some people believe that Earth's future lies closer than that: on Mars. NASA plans to send a human mission to Mars by 2014. Robert Zubrin thinks we need to go sooner. Zubrin and seven hundred others founded the Mars Society in 1998. Their goal is to have the first people on Mars by 2010. They believe we must go to Mars to learn more about Earth and the solar system. They also believe that "civilizations, like people, thrive on challenge and decay without it."[7] They believe that settling a new planet will give people an opportunity to start over. And they believe that a Mars program "would challenge young people everywhere to develop their minds to participate in the pioneering of a new world."[8]

What Lies Ahead?

These plans for the future raise the same questions humans have faced for the past fifty years. Every

How NASA Spends Its Money

Human Space Flight: $5,511,000,000 (41%)

Includes:
- ✓ space station
- ✓ US/Russian cooperative program
- ✓ space shuttle program
- ✓ payload and utilization operations

Science, Aeronautics, and Technology $5,457,400,000 (40.5%)

Includes:
- ✓ space science (Mars surveyor, other unstaffed operations)
- ✓ life and microgravity sciences and applications (space medicine, biomedical research)
- ✓ earth sciences (EOS—Earth Observing System, GLOBE—Global Observations to Benefit the Environment)
- ✓ aeronautics and space transportation technology (research into new kinds of space vehicles)
- ✓ mission communication services (mission control, ground network)
- ✓ academic programs (education)

Mission Support $2,476,600,000 (18.4%)

Includes:
- ✓ safety
- ✓ quality assurance
- ✓ telecommunications

Inspector General $20,000,000 (.1%)

Includes:
- ✓ making sure NASA's administration is operating economically and effectively
- ✓ preventing and detecting fraud and mismanagement

Total NASA Budget for Fiscal Year 1999: $13,465,000,000

Source: "NASA FY 1999 Budget Briefing," NASA, February 2, 1998, <http://www.nasa.gov/budget/99budget_summary.htm> (August 13, 1999).

The Meaning of Space Exploration

discussion of space exploration comes back to technology, money, benefits, risks, and vision. Everyone seems to have a different idea about which elements are most important. And everyone seems to have a different idea about what we should focus our efforts on. Maybe it will be sending humans to Mars. Maybe it will be starting a working colony on the Moon. Maybe it will be finding an Earth-like planet or sending a robot to another star or even sending humans beyond the solar system.

Whatever it is, people seem to be compelled to explore and expand our boundaries. When we explore space, we ask ourselves about some of the great mysteries of life. How did the universe begin? Where did the solar system come from? Are humans alone, or is the universe teeming with life?[9] Maybe we'll find the answer to these questions, maybe we won't. Or maybe space exploration will give us answers to questions we haven't even thought of asking yet.

Every year brings new knowledge about space. The discussion over the future of space exploration will certainly continue. Some people will always want to see Earth's limited resources used to make life better on Earth. Others believe that spending money to solve problems at home is only part of what people really need. As one writer observed, "We need vision, a chance to reach beyond our grasp. Space exploration takes us outside of our surroundings and gives us perspective."[10]

Chapter 1. Beyond Earth

1. Valerie Neal et al., *Spaceflight: A Smithsonian Guide* (New York: Macmillan Press, 1995), p. 127.

2. Quoted in Priit J. Vesilind, "Why Explore?" *National Geographic*, vol. 193, no. 2, February 1998, p. 41.

3. Quoted in T. A. Heppenheimer, *Countdown: A History of Space Flight* (New York: John Wiley & Sons, 1997), p. 185.

4. Howard E. McCurdy, *Space and the American Imagination* (Washington, D.C.: Smithsonian Institute Press, 1997), p. 74

5. Gregg Maryniak, "How Space Colonies Could Benefit Earth," in *Space Exploration: Opposing Viewpoints* (San Diego: Greenhaven Press, 1992), p. 23.

6. Ibid., p. 45.

7. Thomas R. McDonough interviewed by Barry Karr, "Search for Extraterrestrial Intelligence, in *Space Exploration, Opposing Viewpoints*, p. 19.

8. McCurdy, p. 1.

9. Ibid., p. 196.

10. Robert L. Forward, "Technological Limits to Space Exploration," in *Where Next, Columbus?* (New York: Oxford University Press), p. 172.

11. Ibid., p. 193

12. Jane Opalko, "Our Place in Space," *Science World*, vol. 52, no. 8, January 12, 1996, p. 9.

13. Ibid.

14. Ibid.

15. Carl Sagan, "Explorers," in *Where Next, Columbus?*, p. 160.

16. Ibid., pp. 168–169.

Chapter 2.   The Space Race

1. Valerie Neal et al., *Spaceflight: A Smithsonian Guide* (New York: Macmillan Press, 1995), p. 76.

2. Ibid., p. 76.

3. Roger Launius, *NASA: A History of the U.S. Civil Space Program* (Malabar, Fla.: Krieger Publishing Company, 1994), p. 155.

4. T. A. Heppenheimer, *Countdown: A History of Space Flight* (New York: John Wiley & Sons, 1997), p. 129.

5. Ibid., p. 125.

6. Ibid., p. 127.

7. Launius, p. 26.

8. Ray Spangenburg and Diane Moser, *Opening the Space Frontier* (New York: Facts On File, 1989), p. 43.

9. Spangenburg and Moser, p. 42.

10. Public Papers of the Presidents of the United States: John F. Kennedy, 1961 (Washington, D.C.: Government Printing Office, 1962), p. 404.

11. Heppenheimer, p. 218.

12. Michael M. Abrams, "To Aldebaran and Beyond," *Discover*, January 1998, p. 75.

Chapter 3.   Risks and Costs

1. T. A. Heppenheimer, *Countdown: A History of Space Flight* (New York: John Wiley & Sons, 1997), p. 199.

2. Ibid., pp. 263–264.

3. Roger Launius, *NASA: A History of the U.S. Civil Space Program* (Malabar, Fla.: Krieger Publishing Company, 1994), p. 87.

4. Ibid., p. 87.

5. Valerie Neal et al., *Spaceflight: A Smithsonian Guide* (New York: Macmillan Press, 1995), p. 151.

6. Glennda Chui, "Fate of Space Travel Linked to *Mir* Repairs," *San Jose Mercury News*, July 28, 1997, p. 1A.

7. Jeff Cole, "New Space Missions to Test U.S.'s Stomach for Risks," *Wall Street Journal*, November 18, 1997, p. A24.

8. Ibid.

9. Judy Gross, "Plutonium-in-Space Plans Condemned," *National Catholic Reporter*, vol. 33, no. 37, August 29, 1997, p. 16.

10. "Saturn Bound," *Current Events*, vol. 97, no. 10, November 14, 1997, p. 2.

11. Rae Corelli, "The Outer Space Detectives," *Maclean's*, October 14, 1996, p. 66.

12. "The Physiological Effects of Weightlessness," in "Space Program's Future," *CQ Researcher*, vol. 3, no. 48, December 24, 1993.

13. Ibid.

14. Ibid.

15. Ibid.

16. Chris Hayhurst, "Garbage in Orbit," *E*, vol. 7, no. 2, March–April 1996, p. 14.

17. Ibid.

18. Ibid.

19. Walter A. McDougall, . . . *the Heavens and the Earth: A Political History of the Space Age* (New York: Basic Books Inc., 1985), p. 393.

20. Jim Lovell, "Nourishing Today's Space Program Means Bountiful Harvests Tomorrow," *Knight-Ridder/Tribune News Service*, June 23, 1998, p. 623.

Chapter 4.   Is Space Exploration Worth Its Risks and Costs?

1. "NASA Technology Spinoffs," *NASA Facts FS-JSC-95(08)-004*, August 1995, <http://www.jsc.nasa.gov/pao/factsheets/factsheets/spinoffs.html> (August 19, 1999).

Chapter Notes

2. Howard E. McCurdy, *Space and the American Imagination* (Washington, D.C.: Smithsonian Institution Press, 1997), p. 207.

3. Ibid., p. 229.

4. Stephen Jay Gould, "A Plea and a Hope for Martian Paleontology," in *Where Next, Columbus?* (New York: Oxford University Press), p. 111.

5. "International Space Station Factbook," *NASA*, July 1999, <http://spaceflight.nasa.gov/station/reference/issfact.book.pdf> (August 31, 1999).

6. Ibid.

7. Daniel Goldin and Carl Sagan, "The Future of Planetary Exploration," *Engineering and Science*, Winter 1993, pp. 14–31.

8. Quoted in editorial, *New Orleans Times-Picayune*, January 9, 1998, p. B6.

9. "New Millennium Program," *NASA Facts*, n.d., <http://www.jpl.nasa.gov/newmill.pdf> (September 9, 1999).

10. "Center for Space Microelectronics Technology," *NASA Facts, Jet Propulsion Laboratory*, June 1997, <http://www.jpl.nasa.gov/facts/csmt.pdf> (August 19, 1999).

11. "How About a Vacation in Outer Space?" *USA Today* magazine, vol. 126, no. 2627, August 1997, p. 13.

12. John Stamper, "Group Looks to Tourism in Space," *San Jose Mercury News*, March 27, 1998, p. 3DD.

13. "How About a Vacation in Outer Space?" p. 13.

14. Stamper, p. 3DD.

15. Sharon Begley, "The New Celestial Capitalists," *Newsweek*, vol. 131, no. 1, December 29, 1997, p. 70.

16. Ibid.

Chapter 5. The Meaning of Space Exploration

1. Neil de Grasse Tyson, "Space: You Can't Get There from Here," *Natural History*, vol. 107, no. 7, September 1998, p. 75.

2. Walter Kistler, "Humanity's Future in Space," *Futurist*, vol. 33, no.1, January 1999, p. 43.

3. Tyson, p. 78.

4. Alex Salkever, "A Renaissance in the Search for Planets," *Christian Science Monitor*, vol. 91, no. 44, January 29, 1999, p. 1.

5. Ibid.

6. Kistler, p. 43.

7. "Founding Declaration of the Mars Society," *The Mars Society*, August 13–16, 1998, <http://www.marssociety.org/founding_declaration.asp> (August 19, 1999).

8. Ibid.

9. Howard E. McCurdy, *Space and the American Imagination* (Washington, D.C.: Smithsonian Institution Press, 1997), p. 109.

10. "Martian Chronicle," editorial, *San Jose Mercury News*, July 8, 1997, p 6B.

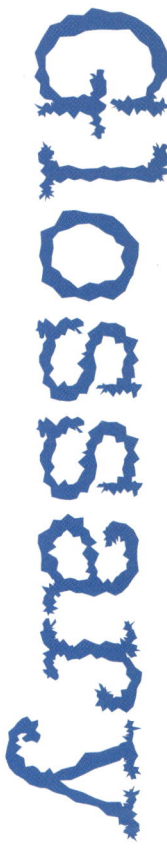

asteroid—A small, rocky body that orbits the Sun. The orbits of most asteroids in the solar system pass between the planets Mars and Jupiter.

astronaut—A person who is trained to travel in a spacecraft to outer space.

communism—An economic and political system based on the concept that all property, goods, and services belong to the society rather than to individual people.

cosmonaut—A Soviet astronaut.

cosmos—The whole universe.

ecosystem—All the living things and their environment in a certain area. Earth's *ecosystem* is made up of all its plants, animals, and other organisms, as well as rainfall, soil and water composition, sunlight, and so on.

entrepreneur—A person who organizes, operates, and assumes the risk for a business venture.

extraterrestrial—Outside Earth.

galaxy—A group of many millions of stars and planets. There are millions of *galaxies* in the universe. Earth's solar system is part of the Milky Way galaxy.

interstellar—Among the stars. Interstellar travel is travel from one solar system to another.

microbe—A living thing so small it cannot be seen without a microscope. The term is usually used for microorganisms that cause disease.

orbit—The path of any body as it moves in a circle around another body. The *orbit* of Earth around the sun takes 365 days. The orbit of a spaceship around Earth takes about ninety minutes.

propulsion—The process of moving something forward.

Space Exploration

rocket—A device that is moved forward at great speed by the force of burning gases being released at the rear. Space vehicles are powered by rocket engines.

satellite—Any body that revolves around another large body in space. The Moon is a *satellite* of Earth. An *artificial satellite* is a human-made object put in orbit around Earth or any other planet. Most artificial satellites provide weather information, send radio and TV signals, or collect information on conditions in space.

solar—Relating to the Sun or another star.

solar system—A star, such as the Sun, and the planets that revolve around it.

Books

Cozic, Charles P., ed. *Space Exploration: Opposing Viewpoints*. San Diego: Greenhaven Press, 1992.

Kennedy, George P. *The First Men in Space, World Explorers Series*. New York: Chelsea House, 1991.

Kettlekamp, Larry. *Living in Space*. New York: Morrow Junior Books, 1993.

Smith, Howard E. *Daring the Unknown: A History of NASA*. San Diego: Harcourt, Brace Jovanovich, 1987.

Spangenburg, Ray, and Diane Moser. *Living and Working in Space*. New York: Facts On File, 1989.

———. *Opening the Space Frontier*. New York: Facts On File, 1989.

Stott, Carole. *Space Exploration*. New York: Dorling Kindersley, 1997. (August 13, 1999).

Web Sites

NASA. August 13, 1999. <http://www.nasa.gov> (August 13, 1999).

NASA: International Space Station. August 6, 1999. <http://station.nasa.gov/station/index.html> (August 13, 1999).

National Space Society On-Line. 1998–1999. <http://www.nss.org> (August 13, 1999).

A
Aldrin, Buzz, 22, 46, 48
Anders, William, 22
animals in space, 18–20
Apollo program, 22, 27–28, 39
Armstrong, Neil, 22

B
Benson, James, 48
Borman, Frank, 22

C
Carter, Jimmy, 39
Cassini Saturn probe, 25, 28, 30
Chafee, Roger, 27
Challenger, 5–6, 26, 28
Cold War, 14–15, 39, 40

D
deaths, 5–6, 26, 27

E
Eisenhower, Dwight D., 15
Explorer 1 satellite, 18
extravehicular activity (EVA), 21–22

G
Gagarin, Yuri, 20
Galileo probe, 24
Gemini program, 21, 22
germs, 30–31, 33
Goldin, Daniel, 28, 42, 43, 48
Grissom, Virgil "Gus", 27

H
Hubble Space Telescope, 12, 37, 51

I
International Space Station, 40, 42

J
Johnson, Lyndon, 6, 17
Jupiter, 24

K
Kennedy, John F., 6, 21

L
Leonov, Alexei, 21, 22
Lovell, James, 22, 36

Lucid, Shannon, 31
Lunar Prospector, 42, 43–44

M
Mars, 7, 8, 12, 24–25, 31, 43, 46, 53, 55
Mars Observer probe, 24–25
Mars Pathfinder, 12, 25, 43
McAuliffe, Christa, 5
Mercury Program, 18, 20, 21
microcraft, 45
Mir space station, 22, 28, 31, 40
Moon, 6, 7, 8, 9, 15, 21, 22, 27, 31, 39, 42, 46, 47, 48, 50, 55

N
National Aeronautics & Space Administration (NASA), 15, 18, 21, 22, 24, 27–28, 30, 34, 38, 40, 42, 45, 46, 48, 50, 53

R
Ride, Sally, 7
robots, 8, 11–12, 36–37, 42, 43, 48, 50, 55
rocketry, 8, 11

S
Sagan, Carl, 13, 43
Salyut 1 space station, 22, 40
Saturn, 24, 25, 28, 30
Search for Extraterrestrial Intelligence (SETI), 7–8
Shepard, Alan, 20–21
Skylab space station, 22
Sojourner, 25, 43
Soyuz spacecraft, 26–27, 40
space shuttle, 5, 12, 22, 28, 34, 40
Sputnik satellites, 14, 15, 17, 18–19, 34

T
Tereshkova, Valentina, 21

V
Vostok program, 18
Voyager probes, 24

W
White, Edward, 27